Mastering Podcasting For Beginners

How to Start a Profitable Podcasting Business from Home

SHASHA

TAYLOR

Copyright

Shasha Taylor
ISBN: 9798652452001
ChurchGate Publishing House
USA | UK | Canada
© Churchgate Publishing House 2020

Table of Contents

Chapter 1

Introduction

THE CONCEPT OF PODCASTING AND WHY MORE PEOPLE ARE LISTENING TO PODCASTS

Podcasting simply means the preparation and deployment of audio files, utilizing RSS to the computers of subscribed users. These files can then be uploaded to multimedia or digital music players like the iPod. A podcast can be simply made from a digital audio file. The podcaster saves the file firstly as an MP3, after which he uploads it to the website of a service provider. The MP3 file gets its URL which, is inputted into an RSS XML document as an enclosure within an XML tag.

Immediately a podcast has been created; it can be registered or documented with content aggregators, such as ipodder.org or podcasting.net, for inclusion in podcast directories. Persons can browse through the different categories or subscribe to certain podcast RSS feeds, which will automatically download to their audio players when they next link-up. Although podcasts are generally audio files made or created for digital music players, similar technology can be utilized to prepare and transmit text, images, and video to any capable device.

Podcasts can be said to be similar to TiVo because it permits users to listen to their chosen podcasts whenever they like, similarly to the way time-shifting allows viewers to see television programs when it suits them. Furthermore, because of the moderate size of the player devices, users can listen to audio files right from the internet as they go about their daily endeavors - for instance, while commuting or just walking around.

However, content creators are massively running to podcasting as a cheap and user-friendly new distribution channel that has the possibility to reach a large audience. Expectantly, bloggers and musicians are prevalent among the early adopters and users, but mainstream media organizations, including National Public Radio and ZDNet are starting to venture into podcasting as well. However, the term originates from a combination of the words iPod (a personal digital audio player created by Apple) and broadcasting. Although the term is created from iPod, you don't necessarily need an iPod to listen to a podcast. You can virtually utilize any portable media player or your computer.

Dissimilar to internet radio, users don't have to tune in to a specific broadcast. Rather, they download the podcast on demand or probably subscribe through an RSS (Really Simple Syndication) feed, which downloads the podcast to their computers automatically.

However, the use of podcast is on the increase and more people are listening to podcasts because of the following reasons:

- **Podcasts make information personal**

The content in a podcast is passed across directly to you, either via video or verbally. That's a very intimate manner of getting information than accessing and reading it from a document or an e-mail.

- **Podcasts are easy to consume; thus, more convenient.**

New podcasts are automatically downloaded to your computer just as they are available once you subscribe to a podcast feed. You can thus listen to them at your convenience.

- **Podcasts are cheaper**

Podcasts are delivered digitally; hence, they cut many costs associated with other forms of communication via printing, postage, and paper. They can also reduce email storage and meeting costs. They are quite easy to archive and updating them is easy and quick.

- **Podcasts are moderate in size**

If your computer is portable, and a podcast resides on it, you can do whatever you desire with it. You can also take the podcasts with you and listen wherever and whenever you desire. Or you can transfer the podcast to a personal media player such as an iPod.

- **Podcasting is time-efficient**

You can listen to podcasts while you do many other things at home or at work. Some kinds of meetings can be cut off in settling for podcasts, saving much time yet increasing productivity.

- **Podcasting is an on-demand technology**

Users determine what they want to hear, and when they would like to hear it, this simply implies you are competing for their eyes and ears. While on the other hand, this means if they are subscribing to your podcasts, there is a good chance that they are actually obtaining the information you are providing to them.

- **Podcasts are one way to communicate to a variety of audience**

The average blog post is about seven hundred-(700) words, which takes not less than five minutes to read. On the other hand, the average podcast is 35minutes, which invariably translates into 4,550words, the equivalent of 6.5blog posts.

Podcasts do not only allow you to deliver more content to your audience, but it's also delivered in a relatively easy manner.

- **It is easier to produce consistently than blog posts.**

Podcasts permit you to curate an awesome piece of content without having to revise over and again. As a matter of fact, the more casual and interactive it is, the better the connection between you and your audience.

- **It creates an impressive personal branding**

In our world today, having an impressive logo and stunning slogan only qualify you as being average in the digital marketplace. What is most important is the personality of your brand. Podcasts permit your business to not only have a personality, but also a voice.

Thus, podcasts remain a valuable tool for increasing your brand awareness.

UNDERSTANDING WHY YOU WANT TO START A PODCAST

Just as the saying that, "if the value of a thing is not known, abuse is inevitable", podcasts should be opted for when you have known its value and how relevant it is to your industry. If you manage a business or have a personal brand you are striving to build, it's very important to consider all the different ways you can communicate to your audience. Technology is by the day adding to the media of communication with potential customers, as there are consistently new ways of reaching out to people and grabbing their attention.

Podcasts are one new medium that is providing businesses an amazing way to communicate and connect with their audience. However, the popularity of podcasts is on the increase and continues to grow as time goes on. However, research by The Infinite Dial found that there are 51 million podcast listeners in the United States. Obviously, this kind of media is not going anywhere and it continues to be a popular method of speaking to audiences about different niche and industry topics. Podcasts can change even the most boring topics into interesting learning experiences that people are eager to know about. This is just a part of the reasons they are very effective and efficient for businesses and brands alike. Furthermore, research reveals that 15% of people in the United States listen to a podcast at least once a week. With the audience continually increasing, there is plenty of room for your podcast to gain traction and attain success. It is not enough to start a podcast, but it is great to understand why you are starting. The understanding of your goal with podcasts keeps you going while at it.

You should start a podcast for the following understanding and reasons:

- Podcasts create a personalized experience
- Podcasts capture your audience's attention
- They help you build and sustain important network links and connections
- They can open up new financial potentials and possibilities
- Podcasts allow you to position yourself as a leader and authority in your industry.
- Podcasts create a personalized experience

Podcasts are great because your audience gets the opportunity to hear the sound of your voice and come to terms with your thinking patterns regarding whatever your subject is. It also permits them to know you on a deeper level. With text, people can't identify your emotions, and some elements like sarcasm, tone, amongst others, can be lost in the process of communication.

Thus, podcasts allow people to hear your voice, and much more your tone, humor, sarcasm, wit and much more. It further assists you in building an emotional connection with your target audience.

- **Podcasts capture your audience's attention**

Perhaps you own a blog post that takes any longer than 10minutes for people to read, it's not likely they will proceed reading all the way down to the end. According to Salesforce, 3% of listeners only listen to the beginning of a podcast, whereas 42% will listen all the way to the end. Obviously, people prefer information that is easy to consume to a piece of text that will take them too long to consume, which is one of the factors which further assert that podcasts allow you to engage your audience for longer periods of time when you are at it.

- **They help you build and sustain important network links and connections**

Do you know that similar to guest posting, you can utilize your podcast to feature guest speakers who share their experience, thoughts and expertise on any given topic? Though it requires a lot of work to plan out and execute a podcast yet, inviting guest speakers on your show is a great way to expose your audience to various industry experts as well as get diverse opinions and insights on a given topic. Having guest speakers is an awesome way of building networking connections and links because there is a high chance you might get invited to their show in return. This will further spread brand awareness and expose you to a new set of audiences within your niche. Create a list of credible when deciding whom you should have on your podcast. Also, engage guests you would like to feature and reach out to as many as possible. Let them know you believe they would be a great fit for your podcast, and ensure they are okay with you being new and having a smaller audience.

- **They open up new financial potentials and possibilities**

In a recent case study, John Lee Dumas, a real estate agent who became an entrepreneur, was able to increase the income from his podcast, Entrepreneur on Fire, to $46,000 a month. This didn't just happen magically, though. Dumas created a method that provided his target audience with information full of insight and value for free. He made up his mind to teach his audience how to create their own podcast that generates revenue so that its more than just a hobby. In so doing, he was able to build and maintain an organic audience of listeners who sincerely enjoy his content and tune-in voluntarily.

Instances like these are popular for podcast creators if they create content with their audience in mind. Creating content that is relevant and valuable to your target audience will be easy if you know who you are catering for, because you will have all the necessary information to determine their point of needs and solve their problems.

There are, of course, a number of ways you can earn money via your podcast. Firstly, you can decide to charge sponsors to be featured in your podcast, so they get access and exposure to your audience. You can also create ads that are attractive to listeners to check out several products and services important to their needs. You can also utilize your podcast as an opportunity to promote your products and services and inform users why your products and services are relevant and of great use to them.

- **Podcasts permit you to position yourself as a leader and authority in your industry.**

You will be seen as a professional and expert if you are able to gather enough listeners and network connections. People will notice the attention your podcast is getting and trust you for advice, thoughts and opinions. Perhaps it gets more rating, listeners new visitors will be more likely to give your show a chance. Center your content marketing strategy around valuable content to your audience first and foremost.

Ensure you bring novel and fresh ideas to the table in your podcasts. Don't base it only on storytelling or technical content. Bring in different elements, so you cover all areas for your niche in an interesting and fun way.

Thus, in going into podcasts creation, you need to know podcasts help you to get your ideas out to the world in a way that people enjoy. With podcasts, you are able to have a hold on your audience's attention for longer periods of time, create a personalized experience, build and sustain valuable network links and connections and, of course, make a decent income. In conclusion, it positions you as a professional and expert in your niche so that new listeners can look up to you for new ideas and insights.

WHAT NICHE AND AUDIENCE DO YOU WANT TO REACH (RESEARCHING YOUR NICHE AND YOUR AUDIENCE)

You need to treat your podcast as a business if you want it to be successful. For the mere fact that your idea sounds good on paper doesn't mean it has a very strong chance to succeed, and without good research to support your plans, it's not likely you will be able to build an audience. Right before you commence recording content, you will need to set up your studio, ensure there is a reliable internet connection, and create a personal brand to market around. But before any of that, choosing a niche matters- and the main direction- for the podcast, that is, your target audience.

Your niche will be the main focus for your podcast-both in terms of the content you curate and the audience for whom you curate it.

Your niche matters for different reasons:

Brand Differentiation - A niche differentiates your brand from others. There are hundreds of podcasts in high-level areas like 'improving productivity' or 'business development.' You will definitely need something unique if you desire to stand out.

Competition Reduction - Defining your niche is a great way to reduce the competition you would face. The more specific and focused your point is, the smaller your audience will be, but the fewer the competitors you will have to deal with. That means you will have more chances of connecting with your audience, and a better opportunity to build and sustain a loyal following.

Content Direction - Your niche will define what type of content you curate, much more like how a business plan influences how you will run and manage a business. You should be able to make a firm outline on how to generate, build, and develop podcast episodes with a sufficiently detailed niche.

HOW TO SELECT A NICHE

Perhaps you are considering a podcast, and you likely have an overall idea of the type of content you would like to create. For instance, you might want to create a podcast on the topic of entrepreneurship and marketing. But how can you select a specific strong topic to focus on?

Evaluate the competition - Spare some time to review other podcasts in your general space. Put in mind the areas that already have enough coverage, and if there are areas that appear to have no sufficient coverage. Take time to listen to a few episodes of the most popular podcasts in the space; perhaps there is a key weakness you can capitalize on. Do you think listeners are unhappy with the way and manner things are currently run? Look for any sign that could get you a competitive edge.

Brainstorm the possibilities - Begin by utilizing the brainstorming method of your choice to expatiate upon your initial idea. For instance, you might use a mind map to chart out the most important ideas connected to your initial concept, or probably interview people in your industry to examine what topics or focal points they feel are lacking coverage. Draw out a big list of possible ideas for exploration and prepare your mind to generate more. With that, you can go through them when you have gotten more information about the current market.

Carry out your market research - You will need to carry out some high-level market research. Learn to know more about the demographics you are considering targeting with your podcast. What are they like? Who are they? What are their wants, coupled with their needs? And most importantly, are they currently listening to podcasts and how are they listening to them? Perhaps you have the time, consider developing "listener personas" to get a better idea of who your audience members are.

Talk to your would-be audience members - When you know you have a very good understanding of your target demographics, and a lot of possible niche ideas, begin talking to some real people within those demographics. Enquire from them specifically what they would like to hear in a podcast, and perhaps they would be interested in listening to what you have to offer. This is an unmatched opportunity to get first-hand reactions to your initial ideas.

Experiment with outlines - You probably have a faint idea of what you want your niche to be by now. Begin drafting outlines for possible episodes when you are feeling somewhat confident. This will assist you in determining how feasible it is to develop content for this niche on a regular basis.

Consider plans for expansion - If your niche is very focused and specific, eventually, you will start finding it difficult to come up with new content ideas. It is therefore good and advisable to have some plans for future expansion. Can you get another related niche in the future? Can you zoom out to attain more generality once you establish an initial following?

Immediately you have decided to carve your niche for your brand, you can start creating content that will feature your podcast on the map. It is not likely that you will attain success right away, but on your research and commitment to your core idea, you should be able to begin cultivating a following.

Furthermore, the revenue aspect and target audience will help in determining how many episodes you need to achieve your goal. For instance, will your podcast require short episodes daily or weekly long ones? However, more episodes may be fitting for an ad revenue strategy or promotion of your products and brands. Small but frequent episodes may be suitable for strategic partnerships, sponsorships, or a patron monetization channel. The value and effort of podcasting will require you need to be planned.

In conclusion, do primary research as earlier highlighted and know about the concerns and preferences of your target audience. Interact with your business team or people that know your niche. In so doing, you will be able to come up with podcast topic ideas that people will be interested in.

Chapter 2

What Equipment Do I Need?

THE BASIC PODCAST APPROACH (EQUIPMENT NEEDED)

Launching a podcast is not an uphill task, and you won't need much to get started. For the basic level, you can start with just a microphone, headphones, recording and editing software and, of course, a publishing platform to get your work shared. So, for your basic podcast, below are the tools and software that you will want to consider before you commence.

A good microphone

Audio is one of the areas that you can't afford to cut corners with. Though your audience might be able to overlook a lot of issues with your podcast, but poor audio is regarded generally as unforgivable. You will want to avoid the microphone that comes built into your personal computer and rather opt for something like Blue Microphones Yeti USB or Audio Technica ATR-2100-USB. Or at convenience, you could spend a bit more and select a dedicated XLR microphone- like the Samson SAC01, and a mixer, for superior quality and better control over the sound produced. If you opt for this option, don't forget to connect the microphone to the mixer.

Headphones

Although your headphones do not have to be top of the line, however, you should opt for something that is up to the job. At least, you will need to hear what you are saying - and what your guests are saying if you are doing some Skype interviews. So, you need to choose some good, on-ear headphones, like Audio-Technica ATH-M30x. Also, you might need to stay clear of microphone and headphone combinations because their sound quality is usually extremely poor.

A pop filter

Your b's and p's will sound amplified when talking directly into the microphone. You can simply avoid this by speaking to the side of your microphone rather than directly into it, or probably get yourself a pop filter. They are quite cheap and affordable yet priceless.

A Skype account

At some points, if you are going to be conducting interviews on your show, you will want to use Skype. Aside from the fact that this program has excellent sound quality, it is also free. Perhaps your guests don't already have a Skype account; it is easy enough for them to set one up.

Recording and editing software

You will unavoidably need a way to edit your audio. You can as well start with a free program if you would like. Adobe Audition remains an outstanding tool that offers you a lot of options for post-production.

However, GarageBand is another good option and it comes pre-installed on Macs. So, perhaps you are an Apple user, you already have it.

ID3 Editor

Most podcasts and recording software will permit you to tag your podcasts utilizing ID3 tags, but if not, you can get it done easily with an ID3 editor. This will permit you to store important information such as the track number, title and artist in the podcast- and will also permit the album art to display when people download it.

A podcast hosting account

There are a number of amazingly affordable media hosts you can use. Libsyn remains one of the more popular hosting and publishing choices, although SoundCloud and Blubrry can also be checked out.

Design software

A vanity URL

Conclusively, if you are really serious about growing your podcast, you will want to make it simple for listeners to leave you reviews and comments. One of the best ways to get this done is to snatch up a vanity URL. These are links that you can utilize to redirect to your podcast's reviews section on iTunes. This will save you from having to give out a long and complicated website address, making simple the process for your listeners or audience.

When starting a podcast, you really can spend as much or as little money as you would like to get started.

THE ADVANCED PODCAST APPROACH (EQUIPMENT NEEDED)

In order to take your podcast a notch further, equipment needed for a basic production are required alongside some advanced tools for sophisticated podcast production. They include;

A Boom

Although this is not compulsory when you are starting out, a suspension boom to hold the microphone is important if you want to become podcasting professional. Aside from saving you from arm cramps, a boom is also important for sound quality, as you won't have to bother about the microphone drifting away from you as you speak into it.

Design Software

One of the best ways to extend the reach of your podcast is by listing it on iTunes. If you do this, you will want to have a good-looking image situated next to your show's name- cover art. This is the photo that people will see when going through shows or listening to yours. Thus, it matters a lot.

A Laptop

You will need something to take records of your podcasts and somewhere to keep all your raw materials and tracks. A number of podcasters use the Apple Macbook Pro, which gets you up to 10hours of battery life and features an eighth-generation quad-core Intel Core i5 processor for hyper-fast and quite a reliable recording. The 13" model is super thin and lightweight, making it simple to tote around on location.

As a starter, and someone looking for something more affordable, Acer makes a decent 15" laptop with the reliable AMD Ryzen 3 dual-core processor, a ton of built-in ports to easily link together with your equipment, and up to 7.5 hours of battery life. These features are all packed into a slim and slick package for below $350.

A Mixer

According to Intern Chuck, "a mixer is definitely worth splurging on." Whether you are laying tracks, experimenting with effects, or adding background music, the 'FU' guys commend the Focurite Scarlett 18i8 Interface. However, with eight analog inputs, including four Mic preamps, the Scarlett 18i8 is amazing for podcasts that need to record multiple sources at the same time. Two independent headphone outputs allow two people to monitor the recording and mixing all at once, while the sound quality is uncompromised. It is all kept in a sturdy metal case that can handle a couple of humps and bruises without worry.

Recording Software

The "FU" guys recommend downloading Audacity or GarageBand, which change your tablet or laptop into a full-fledged recording studio. Both companies provide free versions of their software, which allows you to record live audio, adjust the speed of your recordings, edit files, cut and splice, and output your podcast to a digital sound file.

A pair of noise-canceling headphones

Include into the equipment list, a set of noise-canceling headphones that permits you to literally plug into your recording. The Sennheiser HD28OPRO, which has a more tight seal around the ears for more accurate, detailed listening without distractions, is a very good recommendation.

However, for a true noise-canceling pair, upgrade to the Sennheiser Momentum 3 Wireless Headphones, which offer you studio-quality audio with more accurate sound transmission. Select from three different Active Noise Cancellation modes, largely depending on your recording environment. The Sennheiser Smart Control app allows you to manage your settings and equalizer from your phone - great for on-the-go recording.

A solid recording space (preferably soundproof)

You can record a podcast anywhere. I have had mobile setups in train cars, backyards, music festivals- anywhere you can think of. I never like the idea of recording in somebody's basement or in some corporate sterile studio or office. There is a certain alchemy that happens when the public can see what is happening behind the glass and it makes the process even more exciting for hosts and guests. However, most renowned podcasters believe that it is best to have a secluded space. To make sure you have a quiet space, consider investing in some soundproofing material, like foam panels that cover an area of 10 square feet and can be easily fixed to a wall.

Chapter 3

Getting Started

The podcast you map out is always going to be better than the podcast you don't. Hence, how do you map out a podcast script?

- **Bracket with promotional details**

Creating one isolated podcast won't achieve much if you don't have a powerful brand. If you have a powerful brand, then failing to take advantage of a recurring podcast would not yield many results.

However, podcasting remains something you gradually build up utilizing various methods, until you eventually establish enough audience that your archive becomes a very powerful tool. Because of this, it is necessary that you include promotional details at two points in every podcast: at the beginning and at the end of the podcast. If you clearly state to your audience, the name and nature of your show as well as your social media details and website address at the beginning and end of an episode, you will have a much better chance of picking up returning and loyal listeners.

- **Preview, content, wrap-up**

Each podcast has a specific purpose around which it is built, and you need to make it clear to your audience. This also involves bracketing, and in this context, it is majorly about setting things up, delivering and even revisiting them.

Opening

Just after your opening promo, you should talk for a short period of time about the subject of the episode:

> ➢ What you want to get across,
> ➢ How you intend doing it,
> ➢ Anything else you think the listener should know about the whole episode.

Middle

You can then move forward to the aim of the episode, covering the topic of the day.

End

This is the time for the post-podcast cooldown. At this point, you might need to cover the highlight of what you have discussed, identifying key actionable takeaways and explaining in detail how they get along with your other episodes.

However, after every part, you should permit a beat to allow things to sink in, and after every main section, you should give room for a larger break. You could fill up that break with general talk about your podcast, important anecdotes or even advertising segments.

From the foregoing, writing a script for a podcast is not so complicated. It is majorly about covering the bases (your branding and episodic structure), then dividing your contents into segments to keep people interested, and give room for contemplation and even advertising perhaps you want to take that route.

CHOOSING THE RIGHT FORMAT FOR YOUR PODCAST

Before you start contemplating where to host your feed or how to get listeners to your show, the first factor you need to consider is the kind of show you will be making. That is, you need to select a format.

While interview shows is one of the most popular formats presently, there are many diverse ways to make a podcast and still stand out. Different podcast formats are:

➤ Conversational
➤ Educational
➤ Interviews
➤ Non-fiction storytelling
➤ Solo-casts
➤ and fiction storytelling (often referred to as podcast theatre).

WHY SELECTING A PODCAST FORMAT IS IMPORTANT

Building an audience centers on consistency. That is, consistency in the topics to talk about in your podcast, consistency in the frequency of posting new content, consistency in the style of the photographs on your blog. And as regards podcasts, consistency is required in the format adopted.

Your audience likes to be aware of what to expect whenever they click play on a new episode. Perhaps your show features a comedic discussion this week, a serious interview the next, and a solo-rant the week after, you will find it difficult to gain traction. In fact, they will not know how to describe your show to others, so it becomes difficult to get new listeners via personal recommendations.

Interestingly, it is fairly simple to settle for a format once you begin brooding about what you want your show to be and the best ways value can be brought to your audience. The most popular six podcast formats are thus discussed below:

- **Conversational podcasts**

Listening to a conversational podcast is likened to overhearing a chat between two friends. These types of shows usually have multiple hosts, and episodes could include discussions on a focused topic or a wide range of issues about life, technology and the internet, amongst other topics.

These types of shows are characterized by the easiness to listen to, record and often tend to be between half an hour to an hour long. Listeners often tune in because they love the hosts' personalities and because it is a conversation they are overhearing, they would definitely feel more connected to the hosts than to those reporting a story in a storytelling show, non-fiction, for instance.

The pros

You will just need a brief outline in place of what you intend to discuss in the episode because of the flexibility of its structure. In case you run out of things to say, there is always someone to bounce off.

The cons

You will need to be creative and specific with the topics you discuss to engage your audience and keep them coming back for more.

You may have to deal with recording separately and editing the tracks together, depending on the location of your co-host.

- **Educational shows**

Educational shows are more structured than a conversational show but often with multiple hosts. The episodes feature a specific lesson or takeaway, and listeners often tune in with the readiness to learn about the topic at hand.

However, learning by listening to a podcast is great because you learn while doing the dishes, commuting, walking the dog. Also, producing an educational show will mean creating ever-relevant content that can be consumed for years to come.

Pros

High-value information will keep your audience glued and coming back for more.

It is easier to create supplemental content like videos, PDF downloads and even full courses to get your audience engaged on multiple levels.

Cons

Without supporting visuals, some topics can be hard to teach.

- **Interview shows**

This is a classic in the podcasting world. In the overall, interview shows feature a consistent host or hosts and a guest at each episode. They offer the audience a chance to be introduced to a whole lot of interestingly amazing persons within a niche and learn from their expertise.

Having a common thread connecting all the guests makes the interview shows work best.

Pros

Minimal editing will be expedient as conversation flows. As each guest discuss their perspective, you won't run out of things to say.

Cons

You will need to add to your tasks, emailing and arrangement of new guests and recording on their schedule. You will be at the mercy of internet connections; perhaps you are interviewing through Skype or Google Hangouts.

You will need to think of an outstanding niche or spin to make yours stand out because there is already an abundance of interview shows.

- **Non-fiction storytelling**.

Just as the name implies, storytelling podcasts are shows that do just that- report on stories from around the world. The stories reported could be epic or news. They can also bring to limelight smaller-scale but interesting stories like the science-based storytelling on Science Vs.

Non-fiction storytelling podcasts remain a great chance to share your curiosities with the world. In opting for this format, you will need to put on your investigator hat as this format usually involve audio clips from several interviews and narration to inform the audience of what they need to be aware of, to get a complete understanding of the story.

Pros

As shown by the viral success of Serial, these types of shows are addictive.

There is a lot of liberty to be creative with editing and production.

Cons

Apparently, a higher production value is expected with this type of show. Therefore, there may be a learning curve when getting started, and shows may likely not be produced regularly.

There will be more research and planning involved as these are not the types of shows where you can just hit record and speak into the microphone.

- **Solo-casts**

Solo-casts feature monologues on an important topic to the creator. The episodes can be based on the creator's personal experience and could be anything from comedy to advice-based content. Your audience will feel a deep connection with you, and you can be free to bring on guests from time to time and then, for added interest.

- **Podcast theatre**

You will love podcast theatre if you love audiobooks or fiction in general. These are, however, fictional stories narrated across episodes like a TV show, but just audio. They feature scripts, actors and just like TV shows; they usually have cliffhangers and intriguing plotlines that keep listeners glued and kept in suspense to know what is next.

Perhaps you are a fiction writer or into producing short films, this could be a great podcast format for you to explore and utilize your storytelling skills in a new way.

Pros

Currently, there is a less saturated market for these kinds of shows.

These shows can be addictive, just like non-fiction storytelling shows.

Cons

This format entails more work. You will undergo all the difficulty of writing a story, including the added work of producing it with voice actors.

It might be a bit difficult to get new listeners to give it a try, as this is a less popular show format.

HOW TO PICK YOUR PODCAST FORMAT

In opting for a particular format, you need to ask yourself the following questions:

> ➢ What do you want your audience to make out, from listening to your show?

Perhaps you want to help them learn; then an educational podcast will be the best option for you. If your aim is to entertain, then a conversation-based show with a funny co-host will work well for you to yield the needed results.

Select a format that will be best to achieve it, whatever your goal for the podcast might be.

> ➢ How can you make your show unique?

There so much room for creativity within each of the formats, and adding your unique style to it is very important. For instance, interview shows remain a common format in the businesses and marketing niche. They permit the audience to learn from others' insights, successes and failures. Nevertheless, this also means if you decide to start an interview show, be prepared for fierce competition as a lot of podcasters are in this niche. You must bring in something extraordinary to standout on this turf.

> What can you do with this common format to enable you to stand out?

Give your audience a reason to always listen to you over the others in your niche. Who knows, this might even mean you combining elements of two different podcasts formats or exploring a differing perspective to your topic that other podcasts don't touch on.

> What format will be most suitable for your personal strengths?

You should consider your strengths and go for the format that best suits your content delivery style and editing abilities, just along choosing a format that best fits your aim.

HOW FREQUENTLY SHOULD I RELEASE MY PODCASTS?

Deciding on how often you podcast is largely dependent on your content. Perhaps you talk about a weekly TV show; then, it's apparent that you should have a weekly podcast. How about considering a semiweekly episode?

What is your topic?

Do you talk about the latest trend, gist, celebrity gossip or technology? If yes, you may consider releasing an episode each day.

Do you talk about something evergreen, like parenting or building a business? If yes, a daily episode may be too much, but you probably gather enough content to release either once or twice a week, or even monthly.

How much information do you have?

How much content do you have about the subject? Brainstorm episode ideas and consider how many of those episodes are good enough to produce in the year? Identify your number of ideas and breakdown how often you can get those ideas published. Perhaps you have 50solid ideas; having your podcast published once in a week sounds right about 100. Thus, you may be able to accomplish two each week.

What is your schedule like?

What can you handle realistically? Take your time to observe and analyze how long it takes you to put together an episode. Then, put all aspects into consideration. From brainstorming, research and querying of guests right to recording, editing and promoting your episode.

Perhaps you observe a 5-10hours of process and you work 50hours a week, you might not have the time to produce two episodes in a week. Thus, before jumping into more than you can handle, be realistic with your time.

Quality over quantity

Frequent episodes will reveal to Google that you are active, and this might help your SEO. Nevertheless, if your quality struggles because your frequency is too high or your audience can't keep up with your episodes, you won't get many downloads. It might result in you not keeping a steady following and you won't end up with an impressive SEO in the end.

In conclusion, your focus should be on quality episodes, no matter what. This might mean that you will have to publish less frequently, but if your content could be as qualitative as bringing people back, it is worth it.

In the first instance, determine how timely your content must be, then set a schedule and try as much as possible to stick with it. A weekly format seems the most common, and the easiest to hold with consistency.

WHAT SHOULD BE THE IDEAL LENGTH FOR MY PODCAST?

The length of each podcast largely depends on your chosen niche and how frequently you wish to put out content. Unless you have a highly loyal following, releasing one-hour episodes every day could be an over-kill. Perhaps a subscriber goes on a week vacation; they will return to meet five hours of content, which can make catching up extremely difficult.

On the other hand, a monthly podcast shouldn't necessarily be a two or four-hour-long episode. It's okay if much content are recorded but broken into smaller episodes to make it easier on your listeners. The more frequently you get your site updated, the more Google will love you and the easier it becomes to build a faithful audience. However, based on findings and opinions from listeners, the following episode lengths are recommended:

Podcast frequency	Episode length
Semi daily	1-5minutes
Daily	1-15minutes. (it could be 30)
Weekly	15-60minutes. (with some exceptions)

Biweekly   60minutes

Monthly   60-90minutes

Chapter 4

Bringing Your Concept to Life

MAKING EFFECTIVE INTRODUCTIONS

The introductory part of your podcast episodes could turn listeners away from your podcast if not done to keep them glued. Your podcast opening is how you start your podcast. This entails everything the listener hears right from when they press play to when you start sharing your prepared content. The potential elements of a podcast opening are:

Podcast Name - This is compulsory as it lets people know what podcast they are listening to.

Episode Number - This is necessary for chronological reasons, and it makes redirecting easier.

Episode Title - Perhaps your title gives an insight into the content of your episode, then do well to include it in your recording.

Sound Effects or Music - Opt for something other podcasters are not using. This helps single you out.

Hosts' Names - You will agree that listeners should know who you are. Then, introducing yourself as 'I am........' rather than 'My name is _____.'

Podcast Explanation/Tagline - Don't forget to explain the purpose of your podcast or its tagline, which, however, should be a shortened form of your purpose. Thus, don't assume all listeners know what your podcast is all about.

Introduction/summary - If appropriate, let your audience know what you are going to talk about.

Network ID - You are expected to state it in some way, perhaps you are a member of a network.

Recorded Date - This should be done only if your content is current-event related or time-sensitive.

Sponsors - It is necessary to recognize the people who help you to clear the bills, or your product or service.

Disclaimer - Perhaps your content is for a mature audience, you desire to share a spoiler-filled or spoiler-free review of a movie, or other reasons, make it compulsory to add a disclaimer as early as possible.

However, of these eleven elements, the first six or seven should be included in your opening for every episode.

HOW TO INTERVIEW AND MAKE GUESTS COMFORTABLE

Hosting a podcast interview is not as easy as it sounds. It is not as easy as having a friendly chat at the front of a pair of microphones, as you might end up having a boring interview if you don't prepare well. The steps to having an interesting interview and of course, making your guests comfortable are thus discussed:

Select interesting guests.

Some guests could be boring and some are not just right for your show. If you interview people who don't add value to your listener's lives, you are most likely to host a terrible podcast interview.

Invite guests who do things differently or refuse to follow the norm. Guests who overcame unexpected or unique challenges and possessed unique angles are the right spec. You will struggle to keep your listeners engaged if you interview regular people who just punch the clock every day.

Carry out some background research on your subject

You should know a little about your subject before the show starts. Since your job is to expose the interviewee to your audience, it helps to know enough about the subject to keep the conversation rolling.

You can do well to dig into your guest's online presence. Read through their articles, go through their social media profiles, and search around for what they have said online, what others have said about them, and their opinion on sensitive issues. Also, take note of their big accomplishments like, if they have a published book or won an award in areas pertaining to the topic.

Know your interviewee's works

You should get yourself familiar with your interviewee's works. You should see their videos, read their blog posts, check out their social media pages, and listen to podcasts they have been featured. Perhaps, they have a book, read through, or at least the relevant parts.

You can go further to listen to your guest's most recent interviews, take note of the questions they are regularly asked and try as much as possible to avoid them. Find your angle and get questions that will place a demand on them to provide unique answers, because you can't afford to let your interviews sound like every other one they have given.

Write the guests' bio.

Most guests have a bio prepared for any use: a statement about what they do, where they studied, where they have worked, and what they are currently working on.

Perhaps you ask your guest something like, "tell us about yourself," they will straight away give you their prepared bio. In most cases, these bios are often long and boring, and at other times, they are too short and don't add much.

Thus, it will be wise of you to prepare the guest's bio from your research on them. You can browse through their social media pages, read the 'ABOUT' segment of their website and use what you learned from your research. Most importantly, write the bio having your audience at heart. That is, select the elements that are most relevant to your audience.

Determine where your subject meets your audience

Since your podcast interview is for your audience, it is expedient you determine what your interviewee knows that appeals to your listener's interest. There is no point going over things your audience already knows or things they blatantly don't care about. Thus, you have to extract information that matters the most to your listeners from your guests.

Prepare your questions in advance

You don't need to prepare every word you will say, but it is necessary to have a core list of questions you intend to ask. However, don't be afraid to veer off your planned course during the interview. Sticking to the prepared questions might make your conversation look too artificial. Thus, your need to respond to your guest with genuine questions extracted from their responses cannot be over-emphasized.

To develop questions, here are a few tips:

- ➢ Don't ask YES/NO questions
- ➢ Don't ask basic questions
- ➢ Don't ask a leading question
- ➢ Ask one question at a time
- ➢ Don't in any way refer to your list of questions.
- ➢ Concentrate on 'how' and 'why' questions
- ➢ Start from the beginning. That is, avoid asking your juiciest question first.
- ➢ Send your questions to the guest prior to the interview

Send your questions to your quest at least a week before you get the episode recorded. This will offer them enough time to organize smart responses. They may either choose to simply think about their answers in their head or write out detailed responses. Either way, this approach will make them more comfortable and, thus, help you create better content.

Tell your guest about your show

Your show will be better if your guest knows a little about the show and your audience. You can send a brief email that explains:

➢ Your podcast style

➢ Your typical listener/ audience

➢ How much of their time you will need

➢ How you intend to promote the episode.

This will ensure there are no surprises that could shake your guest off their feet and also help them tailor their responses to your audience.

Minimize distractions

Ensure you have nothing else going on at the time when you invite someone to have a conversation for your podcast. Do whatever you can to sustain the guest's attention.

TECHNIQUES FOR WRITING SCRIPTS FOR YOUR PODCASTS

Preparing for your podcast before each episode is an important step. You will need to gather your thoughts, have topics prepared alongside every other information you need to enable you remain focused as you move through your podcast episode. A great way to prepare, however, is to create a podcast script. A script is necessary because it saves you editing time after you have recorded, and perhaps you have a co-host or guest, it saves you if you ever lose your train of thoughts or run out of things to say. Discussed below are the tips for writing a podcast script.

- **Write script for speaking**

Write your script for how you speak to keep it natural-sounding. Write it in your voice and with the flow of your mind. You can read out loud what you write to check if it actually flows in speaking the way that you imagine. Also, ensure you incorporate your personality into your script. Don't get caught up in using the right words; your script needs to be you as much as possible. Thus, use the words that you would genuinely use.

- **Paint pictures with your words**

Since your listeners do not have a visual aid, setting the scene for them is essential. This does not in any way mean you have to detail every little thing that you talk about. Be rather aware that your listeners may need the extra description often to assist them in painting the stories, news, topics, in their heads.

- **Keep it concise**

Keeping your script concise gives you the space for expansion and improvisation while podcasting. Reading directly from your script may affect the flow and make the show boring. Rather, reduce reading by including only words and sentences that you really read on your script.

Making sure your scripts are so on point without unnecessary words or sentences affords you space and time to get creative with your delivery.

- **Be flexible with yourself**

This is connected to writing your script as if it is going to be spoken aloud. Perhaps there are specific words that you like to use, include them on your script, and the same applies to certain stories, news pieces, topics, amongst others. Also, give yourself different alternatives for vocabulary, news, topics, and the room to explore the thoughts that you have while podcasting. Thus, this flexibility makes your podcast more interesting.

- **Make it your own.**

If you are podcasting by yourself, depending on your comfort level with speaking and podcasting without notes, you may need more or less details in your scripts. Sticking to the script might make you a boring host. Thus, get comfortable while on the show, allow it have your blueprint by being yourself and make it entirely yours.

STRUCTURING YOUR CONTENT USING STORYBOARDING

A storyboard is a quick and simple way of showing and sharing your imaginations. It represents a visual way of presenting a story, before actually producing a real video. This gives you a base to work out and further develop your idea.

To keep your listeners glued from the beginning of the show to the very end of it, you will need to structure your content to avoid putting forward all the juicy contents.

To structure your content using storyboarding:

- **Think about the key scenes in your story**

The very first thing to do, when you start working out your storyboard, is to pinpoint the key scenes in your story.

➢ What are the most important shots?

➢ When do you notice important changes or plot twist?

➢ Are there changes in the location?

A very good way is to think about all the key moments of your story. Having a list of this makes it easier to decide how you will like to have them included.

- **Create a narrative timeline**

You should arrange the events chronologically after you have identified the key scenes. Aside from the chronological order, you should add parameters like the time and location when your story took place. This makes it easier to follow your story and prevents you from getting lost.

- **Decide the level of detail**

You might feel overwhelmed by all the details that you need to cover. You can spend hours on every illustration if you are not strict enough about your level of detail. It is often helpful to maintain a practical view on the storyboard and to avoid your team getting lost in the process of interpreting the shots; it is better to keep it simple, and then add some other details later. Reasonably, your storyboard should entails all necessary information and easy to understand.

- **Write a distinct cell description**

The very last step is to describe the action taking place in each of the illustrations. A good way is to concentrate on the most important elements of each individual shot. What action takes place? What kind of setting do you have? What emotions do your characters need to express? Amongst other questions.

TECHNIQUES TO SCHEDULE YOUR PODCASTS AND GUESTS

Do you know all the tasks required to bring a single episode to life and get it properly promoted can take hours, if not days? That is why things like batching your tasks and having a host that provides podcast scheduling are very important for the busy podcaster. Scheduling your podcasts to be released on specified days and time can help to reduce the need to remember to load your new episodes.

To schedule your podcast:

➤ Log in to your RSS podcasting account and tap the 'new episode' icon to add your episode.

➤ Input your episode details, then tap 'schedule.'

➤ Select the time and date you want your episode to be released live, then tap 'confirm.'

➤ Upload your audio and tap 'schedule episode,' when the date and time you have selected arrives, your new episode will go live automatically.

Chapter 5

Collaborating On Podcasts

SHOULD I HAVE A CO-HOST?

Perhaps you are contemplating having someone who will complement and complete all that you bring to the show.

Most times, we are reluctant to enter into a partnership, such as co-hosting. We often get scared of losing the creative control or ending up doing all the work or even messing up our relationship with the potential co-host. Although all these are potential risks involved, nevertheless, there is a magic that is most likely to happen when you interact with someone who pushes you to reach new heights. However, the benefits of having a co-host are explained below.

- **Keeps you motivated**

Partners are often good, especially for rainy days. They can support, encourage and remind you why you started off in the first place, especially at times when you are going off the track.

- **Keeps you committed**

Having a co-host when it comes to podcasting often means you would be more committed to the process of episode creation and you would not lose the zeal and momentum in your efforts to enlarge your audience.

- **Helps with preparation**

Having a co-host means you can now divide the tasks between two people, which would enable you to get through the tasks with greater efficiency and effectiveness, especially when your co-host brings expertise in different fields to yours.

- **Facilitates conversation**

One of the apparent benefits of having a co-host is that they facilitate and enable a natural conversation to take place. For instance, your co-host can ask poignant questions from the view of your listeners, thus assist in drawing your listeners into the conversation and giving room to them to participate and engage with the content fully.

Helps bring balance

A co-host can also bring balance to the table. Drawing from the fact that you both have different temperaments and personalities, and you both function in different situations, can help the show's equilibrium. Also, a co-host might bring out something you omitted in your research or present the topic from a different perspective.

THINGS TO LOOKOUT FOR BEFORE FEATURING GUESTS

To prevent your show from being a flop, be selective as to who gets featured. To avoid boring guests, or one who rambled all over the place, or one with horrible sound quality, here are a few steps for you.

- **Listen to a few podcasts they have been on**

The guest must have been a guest on another podcast. Track their prior appearances and evaluate one or two of their interviews, then provide sincere answers to the following questions:

- ➢ Does the guest have a good sound quality?
- ➢ Do they go off on tangents or answer questions clearly?
- ➢ Do they speak over the interviewer?
- ➢ How much time do they use educating the audience, or are they just talking about how great they are or their product?

- **Have a pre-call**

Pre-calls to screen guests can be helpful. It is always a short, dry run of the interview. It assists in creating the structure and topics of the interview. These calls also help clear up any sound issues prior to the show.

- **Send explicit audio instructions**

Guests who are not podcasters might not understand what sort of set up they need to have a good sound recording. Thus, hosts need to be specific in their instructions. For instance, the host needs to explain to the guest that he or she needs to have a dedicated microphone, not just speak into their laptop microphone.

- **Get their one sheet and ask some follow-up questions**.

A one-sheet is a one-page run-through of the guest and their expertise. Perhaps they don't have a one-sheet, ask them for an in-depth bio. Also, the host can ask specific questions through email or probably in the pre-call and examine how the guest responds. Another trick is to ask if there are some questions the guest would like the host to ask. If the questions they put forward is all about promoting the guest's business, that is a red flag.

- **Be specific about the purpose of the podcast**

Be specific with the guest about what the purpose of the interview is. Often times, it is to educate the audience about a particular topic that the guest knows a lot about.

- **Preparation takes time.**

Proper screening of guests takes time. It might seem simpler to just take the chance and hope the guest performs wonderfully. Nevertheless, screening your guests to opt for the very best finally is always great and rewarding.

SETTLING FOR A STYLE OF INTERVIEW

Worthy of note is the fact that a good interview style can attract potential listeners, but a poorly managed and planned interview might piss off even the most loyal of one's listeners. The different styles of interviews are thus discussed below:

- **Behavioral interview**

This is a face to face interview where questions are asked from the guest, not using words such as 'would' or 'should' but as to 'what the guest has done.' For instance, a guest might be asked to tell the listeners, 'how he solved a particular societal issue or his reaction to an industry-related incident and why.'

- **Case interviews**

In this style of interview, the host puts forward before the guest a situation to solve, generally relating to the subject at hand. The guest is expected to understand the situation and probe deeper into the subject by asking relevant questions and then offering a solution. This style gives an understanding of the business, reasoning and numerical skills of the guest.

- **Situational interviews**

In this case, the host puts before the guest a hypothetical situation and the guest is expected to explain as to how he will handle the situation. Also, a recent happening can be discussed and the guest might be expected to appraise the actions and inactions of those involved.

- **Panel interviews**

Just as the name implies, a group of interviewers conducts a panel interview. The panelists prepare a set of questions that are put forth to each applicant. The panelists take turns to ask the guest relevant questions. They may also decide to put forward some on the spot questions depending on the guest's response.

- **Unstructured interviews**

In this style of interview, there can be planned and unplanned questions and these can vary with guests. Questions are put forward to weigh the guest's understanding and capability of the subject. However, some questions come due to the guest's response to the initial question.

DO I NEED A PRODUCER FOR MY PODCASTS?

As earlier stated, podcasts come in all different variations of genre, style and approaches. Most new podcasters are just looking for a way to have their voices heard by the world and often have no experience being a podcast producer. Probably they have a philosophy or business approach they want others to benefit from, or they have a personal story about radical life changes, wellness, or other topics they want the world to hear.

However, most of these concepts are easy to execute by getting a few microphones, a few pointers on recording high-quality tracks and finding some easy intro and outro bumpers.

But some podcasters want something more than a hobbyist podcasting. They want a creative expression of their idea through more complex structures. When that is the case, it usually requires a lot of planning and preparation ahead of time. It, however, requires someone to have a general vision of the goal of the podcast and be aware of the steps it will require to get the objective completed, and this is where a podcast producer comes in.

The five roles of a podcast producer

> ➤ Creates vision
> ➤ Organize podcast interviews
> ➤ Supervise the podcast production
> ➤ Podcast Editing and post-production
> ➤ Manage the podcast

A podcast producer is someone who has the knowledge and experience in getting the vision of the podcast or probably helps develop it and monitor it through personally or with a team.

However, these roles can be taken on by the host, delegated between a team or sourced out to a committed podcast producer. The question of whether or not you will need a podcast producer will invariably border on whether or not you are up to the task of doing it all by yourself. Perhaps you feel excited and anxious about taking on these tasks, you will likely be able to do it, or at least keep it going.

On the other hand, if you have a vision or concept but feel impossible at the thought of its execution, finding and working with a producer might be of a very great benefit for you and your podcast. If you have someone else to bring on, ensure you have an open conversation about your strengths, your weaknesses and where exactly you will need help in carrying out the vision. Then, ensure everyone's role is well spelled so you can work together for the common good.

Chapter 6

Recording

RECORDING YOUR PODCAST

As earlier stated, you can make use of different software for recording purposes. Audacity is the software of choice for this guide.

- Download the app
- Automatically, Audacity uses your built-in to record. Ensure the one you would like to use is selected from the 'drop-down' menu situated next to the microphone symbol.
- Click the 'input level' bar to monitor the volume level of your microphone.
- Tap the 'red button' when you are ready to start recording your podcast.
- Tap the 'stop button' when your show is at the end.

Did you forget something you need to add to your podcast? Tapping the red button again starts a new audio track right from the beginning. Instead of doing that, pause your recorded audio to enable you pick up where you left off.

When you are satisfied with your recording, package up your podcast by exporting it. Go to File> Export> Audio.

- Add your podcast episode title and select your file type. We recommend either MP3 or M4A (AAC) because they are industry standard and the most common amongst podcast hosting platforms like iTunes.

REMOTE RECORDING

Remote recording your podcast through Skype

A whole lot of successful independent podcasters utilize this method because of its simplicity, reliability and ability to deliver good audio quality.

To achieve this:

When you open Skype using eCamm, a little recorder comes up on your screen and it's as simple as just pressing 'record.' The program, however, records both the video and audio and saves it as a movie file (.mov). Then, you just utilize the tools that come with the program to change that file from .mov to video and audio files.

Also, you can split the audio tracks, which means you end up with one audio file for each voice, which is quite helpful when editing is involved because you have got a lot more control over the audio.

Remote recording your podcast by recording audio locally

As earlier stated, when you are recording on Skype, one person will always sound better than the other will. That is, the person recording the audio will sound better than the person coming down the line through Skype will. One way to guide against this is for each person to record their audio locally, that is, in the location they are. You can achieve this in a couple of ways, but in both cases, you will utilize Skype to look at each other so the conversation can flow as naturally as possible.

To achieve this, both parties listen to each other and chat through Skype but record their audio through a microphone plugged into a portable recorder like an audio editing program e.g. Adobe Audition or Zoom. In the end, you will have two separate audio tracks that will be synced up when editing.

However, you can also achieve this by using eCamm as long as both persons have the program installed on their PC and both hit record at both ends. Finally, the audio tracks are split and the high-quality versions are matched up.

It is noteworthy that when synchronizing the audio after the recording, you will need a visual marker to be able to see where to line up the tracks. The simplest way to do that is for everyone to clap just at the beginning of the recording. Eventually, this will look like a spike in the .mp3 or.wav file and offer you a way to match up the audio.

Remote recording your podcast using a remote recording website

With platforms like Ringr, zencastr and SquadCast, you invite guests to join a session and each person's audio recorded locally and then saved for you to use later.

With Zencastr and Ringr, there is no built-in video, so you will have to run Skype concurrently so you can see the person you are speaking to. But with SquadCast, they have a video built-in into the platform. This website method sounds so easy, but the problem is, this method can get a little glitch if you don't have rock-solid internet.

EDITING

To edit your podcast in Audacity:

1.   Import the audio you have recorded previously.
    ➢ Utilize track one for your main audio track

> Set the audio material in sequence (for example, intro, narration, interview, outro). The audio will display on different tracks when you import multiple tracks. Move it so that all the audio is on one track.

> Leave an empty track underneath for editing

> You will include sound effects, music or secondary audio later in the editing process.

2.   Listen again to your material

Decide on the sections you want to keep or delete and ponder on, if you desire to change the order.

3.   Remove it if you have background hiss, computer noise or other wanted noise.

Utilize the noise reduction tool

4.   Delete materials you don't want.

Delete the material that you will not use.

Concentrate on the large chunks that you don't need for now. Don't bother yet about coughs or other minor noises that you want to fix.

5.   Move everything into the correct order

Utilize the empty track as a temporary space when you move stuff about.

6. Go through the audio and fix all unwanted noises.

Often you will want to delete and close the gap, for instance, if there is a cough.

7. Keep the volume consistent throughout the podcast

Make normal the levels, selecting -2.0 for your peak amplitude.

Amplify any area that is too quiet.

8. Improve the audio quality - This is optional.

Utilize the compressor tool to enable parts sound louder, more 'in your face' softer or so on.

Utilize the equalization tool to change the frequencies, for instance, if you desire to make a voiceless nasal or deeper.

9. Add sound effects or music.

Click on the X to remove the empty track.

Import your sound effects

Delete the sections that you would not be using. For instance, you might only want the first 30seconds of a song.

Move the sound effects/music to the area you desire

Adjust the volume of the music as you wish, utilizing the envelope tool. For instance, you can have the music start aloud, and then become quieter as you speak over the top, before becoming louder again.

Perhaps you are using sound/music throughout the podcast, remember that there are two ways of pasting, the one that shifts everything else on the track and one that doesn't.

Now that you have material on two tracks, you might have to transfer them. You can either move them as one or independently.

Export your finished podcast.

Export it as an mp3 and work on your metadata.

SOFTWARE FOR EDITING

Audacity

Are you a complete beginner who is not looking to spend much money, but has some spare time to know the basics of podcast editing? If yes, Audacity is your best option. Mostly known as a stalwart in the world of podcasting, Audacity remains an open-source audio recording and editing program. Such programs can also be called DAWs (Digital Audio Workstations).

Audacity is the most commonly used DAW in podcasting because it is free. But being free is not enough. It is packed with satisfying features to build any type of podcast episode you desire.

Hindenburg Journalist

This DAW is mainly designed for podcasters and radio journalists. According to the Hindenburg website, the program's focus is on storytelling and the features and designs are tailored spoken-word productions. This feature makes it less intimidating and cleaner than its advanced options.

With this editing software, you can put together complex documentary-style episodes with multiple elements without being an audio production professional.

Adobe Audition (advanced option)

This remains a perfect podcast software option for someone who desires complete control and flexibility over their project.

This DAW has all you need to get to a mastery level in audio editing and production.

However, because of its options and features, Audition can take a lot more learning curve. Nevertheless, once you have grasped the basics, the stuff you can do with your audio is pretty without limits.

Audition remains a standout option if you are ready to spend time and money on getting first-class audio quality with your podcast.

POST PRODUCTION

There are many post-production packages to give your audio the very best quality, amongst which are:

Bronze PKG

This post-production package is a basic package. The audio is imported into Adobe Audition, and the process needed to maximize the audio quality is run. This includes processes like equalization, compression, noise reduction, deverb and any other process that will make improvements on the quality of the vocals.

Perhaps the episode is an interview, the track for each participant would be gone through and one part would be silenced when a party is talking and the other is listening.

Silver PKG

This post-production package includes everything detailed in the bronze package, plus manual editing.

In the course of the editing, every second of the audio is listened to, and the 'ummms', 'ahhs,' and other filler words are reduced. False starts, wet breaths, mouth noise and anything else are also removed. Content can also be removed from the episode, which would necessitate the availability of spec sheets and time stamps.

Gold PKG

This type of post-production package is designed for the podcasters that desire a high-quality podcast but would choose to focus on recording great content, then messing with post-production and show notes.

OBTAINING LICENSE TO MUSIC FOR PODCAST

Purchasing a music license is a sure way to avoid getting into trouble for using copyrighted music. This might sound easier, but bear in mind that not all artists will permit you to use their music and most licenses are only equipped to deal with radio streams, so it could be confusing!

However, to obtain advice on how to sort your podcast music license, you should contact:

United Kingdom: PRS for music

United States: ASCAP

To know about other licensing companies, you can do a quick search on Google and find the right one for your country.

Worthy of note is the fact that pricing is sorted on a case by case level. Perhaps you get loads of downloads, you can expect to pay a higher price than someone who gets only 100-200 per episode.

AVOIDING TRADEMARKED OR COPYRIGHTED CONTENT ON YOUR PODCAST

Copyright is a law that protects a creator's intellectual property by setting terms and conditions under which their work can be used. For you to be able to use their works, creators will probably want you to pay a fee and follow certain limitations and procedures.

When music is 'fair use.'

The fair use policy states that you can use segments of copyrighted material for commentary, reviews and parodies. You might just be using music for fun unless this is the subject matter of your podcast. However, using music for fun doesn't fall under the fair use policy, so you will have to check out purchasing a license. It is also good to keep in mind that the fair use policy can easily be argued against. This reduces it from being a great option.

How creative commons licenses work

This open license permits the artist to set the conditions of you using their music. When something is shared under a Creative Commons license, it states what you can and can't do with the work. This implies that people may let you use their track with no conditions whatsoever; others might want it to be used only on non-profit work or want you to give credit.

Using Royalty-Free Music

As an alternative, you can use Royalty-Free Music so you can avoid all the difficult stuff. With this option, you can use the songs as you please without having to pay a fee. Often, these tracks tend to be made by independent artists rather than big, signed artists.

You can access this option on few sites like; Free Music Archives, Epidemic Sound, Free Sound, and Creatives Commons Music etc.

Chapter 7

Launching Your Podcast

LAUNCHING A PODCAST

Launching a podcast requires hard work, strategies, and a whole lot of planning. However, the six essentials you should have in place before launching your first episode are thus highlighted:

➢ Submit your podcast's RSS feed to all major podcast directories

➢ Finalize and upload at least three episodes to your podcast hosting provider.

➢ Update your podcast's website

➢ Create a pre-launch teaser to generate buzz

➢ Have a launch strategy planned across social media and email

➢ Prepare to publish new content continually.

1. **Submit your podcast's RSS feed to all major podcast directories.**

Immediately you have your podcast RSS feed activated and your podcast hosting account is set up, it's essential to submit your show to all of the important podcast directories. It takes a few days for every listening platform to approve your show. Thus, timing is a very important factor. So perhaps you intend launching on a Thursday, get your podcast RSS feed submitted across each directory on Monday morning.

That offers them sufficient time to review then send the approval link and email.

2. **Finalize and upload at least three episodes**

While there is no precise specification, we recommend you start with three. The aim is to give your audience a great representative sample of your content so they could know what to expect from the show.

3. **Update your podcast's website**

Setting up a dedicated podcast website is essential to the success of your launch, as this serves as a 'home base' for your show. The greatest advantage, however, is that the website will serve as a central hub where your audience can find show notes and transcriptions, listen to new episodes and learn more about your brand. It also makes your show more discoverable. By utilizing SEO strategies, potential listeners will access your podcast episodes in their results as they search for terms related to the show, and thus, aid in growing your audience.

4. **Create a pre-launch teaser to generate buzz**

This step should not be skipped because creating buzz before the official launch can go a long way. For the manual strategy, utilize your network and ask them to consistently post about the show across their social channel or probably leave initial reviews for your episodes. Building this momentum might be the social proof others need to give your show a try when it is officially rolled out.

On the other hand, you can also use the pre-launch contest approach, where entrants are encouraged to share your content through social media or sign up for your newsletter in return for the chance to get a prize. This approach would, however, help build your launch email list and get potential listeners excited about the show even prior its launch.

5   **Have a launch strategy planned across social media and email**

No matter what your niche is, there are two essential channels for utilization when launching a podcast: social media and email. For the best results, try to set up a specific strategy for each and tailor your content to fit each platform. For instance, while posting colorful imagery may work best on Instagram, it may be better to opt for text-based promotion within your newsletter.

6.   **Prepare to publish new content continually.**

When your podcast launch is officially over, it is time to position your systems and processes to continue publishing new episodes and developments for your show. Always keep in mind that the less content you publish after launching, the less opportunity there is for listeners to access and engage with you. Thus, we strongly recommend building out a content calendar and examining if batch-recording episodes is right for you. Having to produce content regularly is one of the biggest struggles for new podcasters, so it is in your best interest to have a clear plan ironed out. This will ensure you enjoy riding the momentum for months to come, after launching with a bang.

EFFECTIVE LAUNCHING STRATEGY FOR PODCASTS

As earlier discussed, the decision to start a podcast should be closely followed by the creation of a podcast launch strategy. A successful launch positions your show up for success and should get you on the radar of your potential listeners. You will need a great sound strategy in place to make sure your podcast has an audience that is willing and ready to help give the attention the show deserves right from the first episode. Thus, an effective launch includes a combination of strategies or approaches designed to build an effective listener base to launch from alongside strategies that keep the buzz alive long after the first episode is aired.

1.   **Build your audience base**

The strategy advocated here is that you need to start growing your audience even before your podcast goes live since your audience will always be the lifeblood of your show. Take some valuable time to evaluate who your audience is, what would attract their attention, and how best to reach out to them. Explore different ways you could grow your audience through the many social platforms available to ensure the creation of a community that is excited just as you are about your podcast launch. Be reminded that your aim is to build a community around your show, and that community should invariably consist of listeners who would gain value from your podcast.

2.   **Get your podcast launch event promoted.**

You should focus on promoting your launch event to build your podcast platform. Creating a sound buzz around your launch event is the most important part of your launch strategy, and there are a lot of ways you can get that done. First and foremost, having a dedicated mailing list built from your website and blog is a great way to start promoting your new show, as the recipients are already interested in your content. Yet, one of the most successful ways to get this done is to promote your show through social media plays, which remains a huge option in building your brand's image and authority. Identify the platforms that your listeners use the most regularly and get those creative juices flowing to get content out that will excite and increase their appetite for your show.

3. **Launch with multiple episodes**

What could ever create a better first impression than you having a lot of valuable content readily available for your audience to listen to? This ensures that not only is your show successful but that it finds success way beyond launching. Putting this into action gives room for your listeners to get to know you and your show before the launching surface, which further increases the chance of them loving what you are putting out, and having them hooked on your content.

4. **Increase the discoverability of your podcast**

You should consider having a written content to accompany your episodes in order to improve your SEO. Obviously, written content remains an effective way to get your podcast promoted, which is why having your own website or running a blog alongside your podcast should constitute a large part of your launch strategy.

5.   **Network.**

You will need to network with other influencers within the podcasting community to help create a buzz within the industry around the launch of your show. Just according to the old adage that says, "it is not about what you know but who you know," you will need to carry out a research to find ways of connecting with these influencers both within the podcast community and with those within your niche, or probably an aligned niche.

Chapter 8

Marketing

GETTING YOUR PODCASTS TO MORE LISTENERS

It is always the desire of every podcaster to get more listeners who would be consistent, engaging and eventually build a community. Here are a few tips to get your podcasts more listeners:

- **Engage your audience**

The aim is to get your listeners connected to the show and to one another when it comes to audience engagement. The more your listeners have a chance to connect with you and their fellow listeners, the easier it becomes to develop a sense of community. To achieve this, you can start an 'exclusive' Facebook group, give shout-outs to listeners, answer listeners' questions and encourage engagement on social media.

- **Cross-promote on your podcast**

Don't forget about other podcasters when you are trying to get your podcasts more listeners. Cross-promotion strategy can be an amazing way to form a partnership with a fellow podcaster, which offers you a chance to add listeners to your audience. Also, another way of cross-promoting is to find a podcaster with whom you share some common grounds and strategize on creating an episode together. This will further help you build your listener base by getting exposed to another podcaster's community.

- **Arrange a meet-up**

Having an engaging listener base is one thing, but meeting one another in person makes a podcast community stronger. Arrange a meet-up and see what happens without bothering about numbers. You might have a very few numbers at first, but with several meet-ups, a sense of community is created, which extends beyond the computer screen.

GROWING YOUR AUDIENCE AND LISTENERS LOYALTY

- **Consistently publish contents**

The podcast audience is loyal if they know when they can tune in to each new episode. Consistency remains the key to growing your audience and retaining the existing ones. It has been revealed that podcasts that publish at least once in a week are more likely to grow a loyal audience that those who are not consistent on the same level. For details purposes, Tuesdays and Fridays are the most common days for publishing.

- **Include keywords in your metadata and audio filename.**

You can employ some SEO tricks to give your content the best chance of being found.

This simply means you have to be deliberate about the keywords to use in your show title, description and show notes pages.

- **Create a new page/post on your site for each episode**

The idea of creating a new or separate page for each podcast episode might sound tiring because of the effort required, yet, the benefits it brings are worth it.

Since Google cannot listen to your audio, it, therefore, relies on all the text information surrounding it to identify the context and value of your podcast content. This also implies that you can keep your audio file, alongside your transcript, show notes and referred resources all in a place, so your listeners can tune in to the audio and know where to access it. Perhaps they want to come back later.

- **Create a high-quality, useful and engaging audio content**

Realistically, your listener numbers will reflect how good your podcast content is. The fact remains that if your content is weak, you won't get the listeners. In the same vein, if you publish high quality, useful and engaging content every week, people will start hearing about you and will subscribe to hear more. Thus, ensure you are producing content that people will want to listen to.

- **Host well-known influencers/guests on your show**

This is a perfect tactic for growing your listeners. By adopting this strategy, you are not only raising your profile, but you are also potentially recruiting a portion of their listenership. Nevertheless, ensure the influencer you are inviting on your show has an active and engaged listener base if you are going to record a boost in your numbers.

- **Optimize your artwork.**

Relevant, visually appealing and eye-catching imagery will aid your podcast to be unique and stand out, and will communicate something about your content to a new audience. To overlook this, is to miss an opportunity to catch your audience's eye.

- **Ask for reviews**

Positive reviews give signals to Google that you are a reliable source. In addition, positive reviews reveal to potential listeners that you are worth subscribing to and will give you a better chance of displaying or appearing at the front page of your selected podcast platform.

There is no point feeling awkward about demanding for reviews. Reviews can be asked probably at the beginning or at the end of your podcast or even in the copy on your podcast page.

- **Get your podcast submitted to multiple platforms.**

You have an option of several platforms on which to publish once you have created your podcast. However, iTunes is the most common podcast app, but there are many others like Stitcher, Google Podcasts, Spreaker, Spotify, Overcast and Podbean - which are also Android friendly. This should be done to maximize your podcast's exposure.

- **Create a supporting video on YouTube**.

You might consider creating a YouTube video to expand your podcast's exposure further while you are publishing it. YouTube is where you will get a huge number of potential listeners as the website with the second-largest audience after Google.

- **Share on your social media platforms.**

Social media remains a powerful method of spreading the word about your podcast. Regularly link to your podcast, and every time a new episode goes live, ensure you link it to your live stories on Facebook,

Instagram or Snapchat alongside your social feeds. Also, always remember to use appropriate hashtags to ensure you are found for the right keywords.

- **Find out where your audience is online.**

This is worth doing though it is a long-term strategy. Without knowing your potential audience's online concerns, activities and behaviors, it would be hard to create relevant content for them consistently. Look to social communities and forums using hashtags that are relevant and get involved in the conversation.

STRATEGIES TO CONNECT TO YOUR LISTENERS

You need to present your podcast in a way that makes your audience feel connected if you want them to keep coming back to your show. This is achievable when you are relaxed but still entertaining and engaging. The following are some tips to help you connect to your audience.

- **Imagine you are talking to one person.**

This remains the most important thing to do when presenting your show, simply because listening to a podcast is not a collective experience for your audience. For the fact that each listener has his/her earbuds in, and doing their own thing, you need to connect with each listener individually. When you are presenting your podcast, avoid as much as possible collective phrases and terms that refer to your audience as a group. Words and phrases like 'listeners,' "ladies and gentlemen" break the personal connection you have with your audience because these words make them feel like they are just one out of many. Thus, there is no personal and deep connection. Each listener wants to feel like it's just you and hanging having a good discussion or probably hanging out. Thus, do yourself and them a favor by using personal pronouns and loving words when presenting your podcast.

- **Visualize someone in your mind**

You have to conjure someone up if you do not have someone sitting across from you. You can probably think about your partner, best friend, ideal listener, or anyone you like. This will help you sustain the energy you might lose when you are not presenting your podcast to anyone.

- **Talk into a mirror**

You can always try recording in front of a mirror to get the visualizing strategy done. Performing to another person or even a reflection of yourself will further help your subconscious channel the social instincts you need to harness your natural conversational energy.

- **Record your podcast where people are.**

If you can't make do with any of the above presentation tips, then try recording where you can see people.

Record in a conference room where you can see your colleagues, perhaps you are at work. Doing this, you would be surprised at what a difference seeing people will make to the energy and output of your voice.

- **Practice**

Just as with every other thing, the more you practice, the easier it gets and the quicker you will find your podcast presenting sweet spot.

If you want to improve, you must listen back to yourself. You would be surprised at much work you still need to do to sound engaging and the only way to figure that out is by sitting where your audience is and listening to what you record. Thus, you will know where you need to be to sound natural yet engaging.

GETTING FEEDBACK FROM YOUR LISTENERS

It is a great thing to get feedback and hear from your podcast listeners-a positive feedback is enough as encouragement on its own; even a positive email or tweet can make all the difference.

Thus, five tried-and-true strategies to get more feedback from your listeners are discussed below:

1. **Make it easy for your audience to contact you.**
Create avenues for your audience to contact you as easily as possible if you want some feedback on your podcast. This simply implies proving clear avenues for listeners to reach out to you. This, however, does not mean you have to make yourself available on all social media platforms. All you need to do is pick the few avenues that you already use in your normal routine and then inform your audience about them.

2. **Ask for responses**
Ask your listeners for responses once you have selected one or two ways for your audience to reach out to you. Ensure you ask for feedback near the end of your show. Don't sound beggy, but let them know you would appreciate hearing from them.

3. **Start the conversation with a specific question**
Asking a specific question, can kick start a debate and get you tons of feedback. Aim for something controversial and somewhat disputed, and create a discussion. For instance, you can ask, what is the first thing you do when you get with a new group that does not know each other?

4.   Let them know you are listening

You need to show your audience you are listening if you want to get great feedback. You are encouraging more feedback every time you respond to a question or highlight some feedbacks on your show. Doing so, you are creating a virtuous cycle of more feedback. Then, make your response, as personal as possible and your audience will love the attention.

5.   Prime the pump

Don't get yourself worked up if you haven't received a voicemail, email or even a tweet yet. Don't because you haven't had an email doesn't automatically mean you haven't had any feedback. It's most likely you have shared your podcast with a family member or a friend. Did they have anything to say? Did they ask any questions at all? If yes, then highlight this feedback in your next comment. It is enough to get the conversation started.

Chapter 9

Monetizing Your Podcast

ADVERTISING AND SPONSORSHIPS

Advertising and sponsorship are popular and effective ways of creating revenue with your podcast. Podcast advertising is quite attractive to advertisers because it remains an intimate format where listeners develop strong bonds with their hosts. About two-thirds of podcast listeners take actions based on the ads they hear from podcasts.

Getting podcast sponsors is very easy, but finding the right ones for your podcast might be challenging, as you do not want to erode the trust you have earned with your listeners by bringing in sponsors that do not align with your audience and brand.

To secure podcast sponsors:

- **Consider your niche**

This is the most important factor to consider. You need to find sponsors that fit your niche to prevent your audience from growing bored and frustrated if your ads are irrelevant to them. You want your ad to fit in your audience so the sponsors can do well too. This way, they will keep advertising via your podcasts and your rates can then be raised over time.

Thus, the very first step is to think about your ideal listener. This is referred to as your avatar or persona in marketing. Fix this person in your mind; their preferences, problems, needs, likes and dislikes. This should also include a short description of the listener, demographic information, and, most importantly, what they want. This would not only save you from serving poisons to your audience, it will also help you craft podcast episodes.

- **Search for potential sponsors**

To get potential sponsors:

➢ Browse through the ads on website or blogs in your niche

➢ Identify companies who advertise in industry magazines

➢ Review businesses that purchase paid ads on social media

➢ Identify brand representatives who post in your online group/community

➢ Search for common phrases in your niche and check out the sponsored slots.

➢ Enquire from your listeners what kinds of products they like and purchase often.

An easy way to find sponsorship is to listen to other podcasts in your niche and approach companies that sponsor them. You can do this using the following tips:

- Don't rule out the little guys
- Don't get too picky about price
- Select sponsors who don't bore you
- Stick to companies you respect
- Be open-minded
- Consider a proof-of-concept sponsor

3.   **Create your sponsorship proposal**

You have to impress your potential sponsors with a proposal that reveals your professionalism and personality. Your proposal should include:

- The title and logo of your podcast
- A summary of your podcast's niche, including episode subject, format, length, and any popular guest you have had on the show or interviews you have conducted.
- Reasonable information about you, the hosts, and anyone involved in the production, including photos and bios.
- Information about your listeners, such as download statistics, demographics, and other pieces of evidence that your listeners love your show.
- Proposed rates and partnership ideas. Clearly state that you are open to their ideas too.

> Your contact information.

4.   **Send your pitch**

Email your proposal to your list of potential sponsors once it is ready. Ensure you compose a quality email because this will be the first interaction sponsors will have with you and your business.

Ensure you explain why sponsoring your show is a great opportunity for them and their audience. To further create some signals that you are very much interested in their brand and products, follow their social media accounts, join their email list and compliment them publicly on Twitter. These little steps would sweeten the deal.

4.   **Follow up with potential sponsors.**

A delayed response does not mean you should abandon all hope. Send follow up emails after your original pitch. Ask them for an answer to your pitch politely, even if they intend to decline your offer.

In cases where your request is declined, end your follow up graciously. Let them know they are always welcome to contact you anytime.

AFFILIATE RELATIONSHIPS

Either you are podcasting for business or pleasure, promoting affiliate products and services can be an amazing way to monetize your podcast.

An affiliate program, however, is where a company offers you a special link or code you can promote to your audience. You may earn a commission when people take action with that link or code. To have a successful affiliate relationship:

- **Seek to meet your audience's needs**

As earlier explained, if whatever you intend promoting is not relevant to your listeners, either by need or desire; it is not worth whatever income that might be attached to it. This further stresses the fact that you need to discover your audience's needs. When you have discovered this, with your recommendations, your audience will be more likely to take action.

- **Promote what you believe in**

It is a form of endorsement from your reputation when you promote something. Even companies are aware that host-endorsed sponsorships are more powerful than ad-insertions, and even preferred by the audience. So don't put your reputation on the lines when you are promoting something. You don't have to recommend what you have used but endeavor to research the quality of the company enough to endorse new things they offer.

- **Become an ambassador**

Promote the product or service as if it was your own rather than being merely a catalog of recommendations.

You can choose to:

➢ Do a review and expound on why you like the product or service, especially why you prefer it to other options.

➢ Make tutorials to show potential buyers how to use the product or service.

➢ Create a landing page that gets your referrals educated on their decision rather than merely pointing them to the product page.

➢ Offer to help

➢ Create a bonus for high-value affiliate/joint venture endeavors.

- **Give simple calls to action.**

Make sure the process for your audience is as simple as possible if you are going to recommend a product. Try to simplify if you have to give instructions beyond visiting a simple URL, and include it in your show notes.

- **Comply with laws, terms and commonsense ethics**

You should state clearly, when you will be compensated for a recommendation because money makes things complicated. Also, ensure you read the terms of your affiliate relationship. You need to know where and how you are permitted to promote your affiliate relationship. In the same vein, commonsense ethics must be put in place. For instance, don't promote adult materials to an audience, don't promote illegal activities or scams or marketing traps.

SELLING MERCHANDISE ON YOUR PODCAST

Immediately you have worked out the method through which your customers would be reached; you need to consider the mechanics of how to sell your products. For simplification, we will divide the options into two categories: those with a service or information to sell, and those selling a physical product.

Service or information products

Perhaps you are selling a course or something that requires downloading. It makes a whole lot of sense to sell it directly from your site and therefore avoid paying any fee. Right on your podcast, you can instruct your listeners to go to a landing page where they would access more information about your product and which you can use for promotion through social media platforms.

Physical products

It makes sense to rely on a sales platform if you are with a physical product because you will be able to take advantage of the feedback section and reach a broader audience. That is, people who don't listen to your podcast but access reviews from people who do. To get this done, you can leverage platforms like Amazon or other creative platforms like Etsy.

Worthy of note is the fact that podcast is a great way of promoting discount codes for your product to enable them to stand out, create chapters during your episodes. However, by segmenting your promotions into chapters, you offer your listeners visual clues, which will further invite them to engage with your products directly.

LISTENERS SUPPORTS OR DONATIONS

Listener support permits you to add a Support button to your Anchor profile. However, any listener can pledge a monthly recurring amount to support your podcast, even when they don't need to have an Anchor account. To activate Listener Support for your podcast:

- ➢ Log in to anchor.fm and navigate your way to your 'Money' icon at the top of your screen.
- ➢ Move to the 'Listener Support' section of the page
- ➢ Tap the 'Activate Listener Support' button
- ➢ Then, you will need to set up a Stripe account and add your payment information to complete activating the feature.
- ➢ Now, search your inbox for an email called 'Welcome to Stripe,' which includes a link to get your email verified and start getting paid.

You will be able to start accepting payments from your listeners once your account is verified. This can take up to 24 hours. You will be notified as soon as it is active. To customize your message to supporters:

- ➢ Go to Anchor settings on the Anchor website and tap 'Money' at the top of the page.
- ➢ Move down to 'Listener Support' and tap 'More Option'.
- ➢ Customize/ personalize your message in the box that displays on the screen.

➢ Ensure you tap 'Save' so your potential supporters can view this message.

To support a podcast:

➢ Tap 'Support this podcast' at the top of the page.

➢ Select the pricing tier you desire to use. The current options are $0.99, $4.99, or $9.99. Automatically, all of these will renew monthly.

➢ Input your name, email address and card information.

➢ Tap to pay at the bottom of the screen.

DIRECTING LISTENERS TO DONATE

There are a number of ways to direct listeners to donate and it is very helpful to utilize several methods to ensure your message about donations is reaching your audience. These methods are;

- **Call to action.**

You can inform listeners that they can donate and request that they do so as your call to action at the beginning and/or end of your podcast.

- **Direct link**

Providing a direct link to donate wherever any information about your podcast is situated is an easy way to make sure your donation information is ace-ssible.

- **Donate button**

Paypal lets you set up a 'donate button' that you can include on your website, in blogs or emails. All a listener needs to do is hit the button.

- **Email list**

Another great way to communicate and connect with your loyal listeners that have subscribed to your email list is mentioning to them that you accept and encourage donations. Also, instead of the general information that you accept donations, you can go a step further to getting it a little more personal and letting them know your plans on the donations you receive.

ABOUT THE AUTHOR

Shasha Taylor is a seasoned podcaster whose contributions and efforts to podcasting remain unmatched. She started her show through podcasting in the year 2012 and since then featured a host of influencers and on her program. She has gone further to groom young presenters and to-be podcasters in the great act of podcasting and voice-over, winning the sponsorship of various big companies and organizations.

She today has millions of listeners and she is an authority when podcasting is mentioned. She had won several awards of merit and recognition to his credit and has written several other books on 'Podcasting'

According to her, she looks forward to further impacting more lives and encouraging folks to pick up a career in Podcasting. Shasha lives in Florida with her husband Romney and two beautiful daughters.

ABOUT THE BOOK

You wonder how you can project your voice, name and contents to the whole world, while you legitimately make money? Podcasting is here to make your dream a reality. No matter your kind of business or content, podcasting has a niche for you, especially now that podcast listeners are over 5million in the USA alone, and still on a daily increase.

We know you have once heard about podcasting but you don't know what it's all about. Worry not too soon, we have got you covered. Do you wonder how to get the big equipment to achieve this? Your headache is over. We have packed in this book how you can cheaply produce podcasts in the four walls of your room without necessarily purchasing big tools and equipment. Yes, it is as simple as that!

You will need to build your channel and a community of listeners through the production of seasoned contents and they would in return help with supports, donations and sponsorship. You wonder how to curate such contents? This book is here to put you through and accompany through every phase right from the equipment set up to recording, editing, connection building and the eventual production and post-production phase! This is podcasting made reality just for you!

ISBN 9798652452001